Teresa Morris Garrison

VOICES FROM NATURE, LESSONS FROM GOD

ISBN
978-1-957895-70-3 (Paperback)
978-1-957895-71-0 (eBook)

This book is dedicated to those who love,
especially my sons Josh and Ben.

Table of Contents

ACKNOWLEDGEMENTS

Thank you to Adrienne for your loving friendship and belief in me. Thank you to Sue for intuitively supporting my work with the nature energies and for seeing this world symbolically with loving eyes.

And many thanks to my dearest ones, my family, who love me and accept me, fairy spirits, gnomes and all. May the blessings of love and peace fill your hearts and lives for all your days here on Mother Earth and forever and forever. I love you.

SAINT FRANCIS OF ASSISI PRAYER

Lord, make me an instrument of your peace!
Where there is hatred let me sow love;
Where there is injury, pardon;
Where there is doubt, faith;
Where there is despair, hope;
Where there is darkness, light;
Where there is sadness, joy.
O Divine Master, grant that I may not so much seek
To be consoled as to console;
To be understood as to understand;
To be loved as to love.

FOREWORD

The Earth is a living being. Humans are a part of the Earth's body much like a cell is part of the human body. The Earth is a part of a larger being, the solar system, which is part of the Milky Way Galaxy. This galaxy joins other galaxies to create another even larger system, the Universe. Universes join universes, growth ever expanding. As humans, you are a part of each of these larger systems or beings through your connection to the Earth. Humans, trees, plants and animals are a part of all that is seen and unseen. We are one.

Just as you connect to other humans through love, you can also connect to the Earth and the Universe through love. Pour your love into every tree, plant, blade of grass, rock and drop of water. The power to transform life flows through your love. As you give love, you grow your capacity to love. Your power to transform expands. Love is the expression of God. Through love you become the expression of God and can change the world.

The emotion of love that humans create feeds the body light substance of the Earth. We trees create oxygen and support the breath of the Earth. Plants transform the light of God into physical energy to sustain humans who complete the circle by feeding the Earth with love. Rocks house energies for many uses such as healing and grounding energy to the Earth. Water is the circulatory system for the Earth, bringing nourishment and cleansing to her and all Earthly beings.

Love yourself. Love others. Love all things seen and unseen. Humans are light from light. Light is the true substance of God. Oneness is light and love.

The Council of the Trees
London

AUTHOR'S NOTE:

I met the Council of the Trees in Kensington Gardens, London. The Council is comprised of nine trees. These trees are long-lived Plane trees and although other types of trees are interspersed in the area, the council forms a sacred grove. In folk lore the plane tree connects the sun and the moon thus creating balance.

The Council serves as elder statesmen in constant communication with all the trees in Kensington Gardens. Through their governance, they stabilize demands on the landscape and resources.

Scientists have accepted plant and tree communication for some time now. In 1979, Rhoades, a chemist and zoologist, demonstrated that trees infested with caterpillars warned other trees and both the infested and unaffected trees were found to have infused their leaves with toxins unappealing to caterpillars. Shultz and Baldwin in the early 1980's placed fifteen poplars in a chamber and ripped leaves from half of the trees. After fifty-two hours both groups of trees had increased their leaf levels of phenolics, a defensive compound. Walnut trees are known for preventing any growth on their land. Anyone who has tried to plant under a walnut tree soon learns this. Trees that are suffering from over-foraging signal other trees miles away to increase tannin levels in their leaves to make the leaves inedible to foraging animals. The Mayapple plans its growth two years in advance based on its analysis of weather patterns.

In India, coffee plantations are mostly created inside forests. Studies have shown that coffee plants communicate with each other and the surrounding trees using a Signal Exchange Language for protection. The language includes drought escape mechanisms and drought avoidance signals.

Some scientists believe trees and plants carefully evaluate their environment, conquer territory and fight enemies. If intelligence is defined as the capacity to acquire and apply knowledge, then trees and plants are intelligent. The Council of the Trees in Kensington Gardens watches over the trees and plants and through communication, all are at one with one another.

1

NATURE DEVAS AND SPIRITS

Deva is an ancient Sanskrit word meaning shining one. Devas function as Nature's overseers, organizing energy to create the natural form of a tree, for example. Before anything is created in physical form there first is a thought or an idea. Energy fuels this thought to manifest the form that we can see and touch. Devas, like architects, hold the thought or blueprint and direct life force energy to materialize the tree and architects, the building. Nature Spirits work in partnership with the Devas and are responsible for maintaining the energy in the specific form. Nature Spirits are like the carpenters working with the architect's blueprint.

Devas and Nature Spirits direct and channel light or life force energy. They perceive a garden or forest as a scene of moving lines of energy. Waves of light from the earth surge through the plants and light also streams down in and around the plant. These waves of light are in constant motion. In our physical world, most humans perceive the plant as a solid. We use our five senses to define the plant. Our five senses are wonderful but limit our experience of the plant's energy as light. Some humans may develop subtle sight and see the waves of energy or auras around plants, rocks and even other humans.

Devas and Nature Spirits, unlike humans who have a body, have no single form. They can make themselves visible to humans and when they do, they choose a form most meaningful and understandable to that human. Although Devas and Nature Spirits have different roles in Nature, I will use the term Nature Spirit or Nature Being to include both. When my experiences with Nature Spirits began, I was too surprised to ask if I was hearing a Deva or Nature Spirit. I am honored to communicate and work with Nature Beings. This communion takes place when I am resonating with the Nature Spirits' energy. I believe anyone can attract and work with Nature Spirits through love with the intention of healing the earth. We are all one.

Om Maha Devaya Namaha
"Om and salutations to Great God" Sanskrit Mantra.
Translation by Thomas Ashley-Farrand

2
THE
COMMITMENT

When I think of Nature and my childhood, I remember facing a huge lilac bush, holding a leaf in each hand, and talking. I no longer recall the conversation. I do remember how I loved that lilac bush. When it bloomed, I would bury my face in it and wish its branches could enfold me. I talked to plants and trees because they talked to me. When I was nine years old my cousin teased me and I stopped talking to plants. My cousin was a boy my age whose skill at teasing was well honed on me. I can still feel the red hot flush of my face and the fear other children would find out and tease me too. Fitting in became my priority and so my conversations stopped and I no longer heard the voices of Nature.

My love for plants and trees never diminished. Grown up, I loved my gardens. I knew every detail of every plant, celebrating the blossoms, new growth and quietly marking the deaths as the seasons changed. In 2003, Nature once again spoke and I listened.

There is no one particular event that opened my ears to Nature's voice. Looking back, the year prior to Nature speaking was one of change. I practiced a prayerful meditation twice a day. I received body work from a healer who used organic essential oils. The essential oils led me to study flower essences, first developed by Dr. Bach. (Appendix C). After using flower essences produced by the Bach Flower Society, I experimented and made my own from the flowers in my garden. I used these flower essences to support and build my light energy. In addition that year I also received my Reiki attunements including the master level. Reiki is a subtle life energy that flows from the Universe, Spirit source (or God) to a practitioner. This energy flows from the practitioner's hands and is directed into another human, animal or plant. This energy is filled with love and the pure wisdom of spirit. Reiki energy creates a healing effect. Each one of these practices enhanced awareness of my human connection to the universal field of energy or light. In that awareness I committed to garden cooperatively with Nature.

In listening to Nature, I agreed to say yes to Nature's instructions and act in faith. I would no longer be the benevolent dictator, The Gardener. In days past, I, The Gardener, made all the decisions. I selected the plants I desired and planted them in locations most pleasing to me. I also condemned plants as weeds and forcefully removed them. I felt no remorse as the small plants I called weeds lay on the ground with bare roots exposed, slowly wilting to death. I, The Gardener, had the supreme right to make life and death decisions in this garden. I relinquished this role to cooperate with Nature. I was no longer in charge. This commitment to Nature was the first step. I had said YES to Nature and to God, which for me are one. I soon learned, to my shock, that I was never in charge. The garden became a metaphor for my life.

> *"Consider how the lilies grow. They do not labor or spin. Yet I tell you, not even Solomon in all his splendor was dressed like one of these."*

—Luke 12:27-28 *Bible, NPV 2002*

May 2003. Before attending a meeting, I sat in the car, eating a hamburger. I looked at a sparse flowerbed outlining the parking lot. Red-brown shredded mulch carpeted the bed. It was dotted with a few orange-yellow marigolds and plain generic green shrubs so popular in uninspired landscaping subscribed by businesses.

"You must make a fairy shelter. The canopy of the shelter is a big flat round rock held aloft by smaller rocks for pillars. Are you getting this? Are you drawing it?"

This was not the usual voice in my head that would be chiding me about now for eating a hamburger. The thin voice that disapproved of hamburgers, french fries and warm soft cookies. The you can never be too thin voice never talked about fairy shelters and certainly not in the loving tone I had just heard.

"You better sketch this. You also will make a raised bed in the shape of an arrow. And put in some small steps to the hosta bed. Some evergreens want to go in for winter shelter."

"Who are you?" I turned my head side to side wondering if anyone could see the spectacle inside my car.

"I am Edward, a Nature Guardian. I am here." His voice was coming from the direction of the car's passenger seat.

"For your understanding, I live under the hostas. Yet I am everywhere. I will help you work with flower essences. I am your garden contact. You ought to get busy. I have been waiting a long time for you. Now the fairy shelter will go to the right of the juniper, just west of the giant hostas."

What is happening to me? This is a different voice and with my eyes closed, I can see Edward clearly in my mind. How can it be that I can see him and I know exactly which of the hundreds of hostas is his?

Opening my eyes, I see he is right there, above the passenger seat, tapping his bare foot. He looks like he is floating on air but he must be standing on something to be tapping his foot.

"There isn't any juniper in the garden."

"I know. I already told you to plant an evergreen. Are you writing this down? There is much to do. I suggest a list. Yes, you look like a list maker. Quick. Quick. Write."

"I am on my way to a meeting right now."

Perhaps not the best response but I was too surprised to make much sense. However, I did write down the instructions. I heard a Nature Being. I even saw a Nature Being. Imagination? No. Crazy? Maybe.

When I made the commitment to garden cooperatively with Nature, I imagined listening to Nature as a quiet intuitive process. Something like "instead of planting impatiens use petunias this year" and then following the suggestion. At the time, I did not know my yes to Nature had no limitations. The yes would not be limited to my idea of a quiet intuitive process, not limited to talking only when I want to listen and not limited to my garden walls. I never dreamed saying yes to Nature would bring forth Edward. When we open ourselves to the universal flow of energy, anything is possible. This I would learn.

Edward had a potbelly. He was not fat but his tummy bulge was clearly beyond any effects of sit-ups, if he did any. Edward's feet were large for his body and very flat as if to have as much surface contact with the dirt as possible. His lime green shirt was neatly tucked into his red dotted pants in contrast with a scruffy, thin beard and fly-away dark hair. His loving demeanor was gentle and yet directive. I questioned what was happening but I did not question his authority.

I drove to the meeting, all the while thinking about what was happening and how this Edward appeared and talked to me. I had not yet made the connection between my conversations with Nature as a little girl and this new experience.

3
THE DANDELION

Before the meeting started, I walked outside to another garden. Hot-pink roses and sunset orange day lilies were blooming against the backdrop of ornamental grasses and variegated greens. In this garden, I noticed a dandelion waving so quickly he vibrated. I first thought what a shame, a weed in this lovely garden bed. The dandelion continued to flutter and vibrate. I began to wonder why it was moving and the grasses weren't. I was distracted as I tried to find a logical explanation for this. How could a breeze move one plant's stem and not others can only inches apart? I recalled an image of me in grade school, waving my hand excitedly in class hoping the teacher would call on me. And so I called on the dandelion. "What?"

"I want to live in your garden." The dandelion continued to flutter excitedly. "Absolutely not."

"Why not?"

"You are a weed, and my garden doesn't have weeds." That was a bold statement. I could not recall one day when the garden was weed-free. Weeds sprouted over night, every night. And every day I removed some.

"You like my yellow blossom."

"Yes I do. You are the brightest yellow I have ever seen in a flower."

"You have always liked my puffballs. Can't I live in your garden?"

"No." Questioning my current reality, I wondered why I was arguing with a dandelion.

"Some people eat my greens."

"That is exactly the issue. You are a weed. You are intrusive and invasive. Where there is one dandelion, others are sure to follow. I do not want so many dandelions in my garden that I could make a salad." I had the last word. I love winning an argument even if it is against a dandelion. Case closed.

We were silent. And I thought of all the plants in the world, a dandelion is talking to me. Why couldn't it be a rose? I remembered my commitment to garden in cooperation with Nature. It would be easy to say yes to a rose. Yet it was the dandelion talking to me.

I took a deep breath and let it out with an audible sigh. "OK, you can live in my garden. But not in the beds where you might disturb the others. You are welcome to live in any of the large garden pots on the deck."

I left the garden and went into the meeting distracted by the thoughts of Edward and the dandelion. I have to pay attention in this meeting I thought. If I focus completely on the business of the meeting, everything will return to normal. After the meeting, all was quiet on my drive home. Days passed and I could not forget Edward or the dandelion. As long as I remembered them, I also remembered this was not normal.

An evening, a week or so later, I was sitting on the deck in my garden, admiring two green pepper plants in a large garden pot. The green stems contrasted nicely with the red terra cotta pot and the soft black soil. I decided to look more closely to see if there were any blossoms promising green peppers in the future. When I looked, I noticed a dandelion in the pot.

Not knowing the right thing to say, I decided it was best to be a gracious hostess. "Welcome. You may live in this pot and I will protect you."

The dandelion was here for a purpose. What purpose? I was curious why the dandelion wanted to be in my garden. I thought about this for several days. Then I remembered I can talk to Edward. I asked Edward to reveal the dandelion's gift.

The gift was the awareness of judgments. How many people cross my path and I see dandelions? When I look inside myself what dandelions do I see? Awareness comes before action. To let go of judging others, I must first see myself in the act of judging. I am judgmental. Things are good or bad, right or wrong, sweet or sour, thick or thin. This list never ends. It is a natural tendency for us to judge. Judging can serve us well. The judgment about a dark alley can protect us. However, our judgments can also diminish ourselves and others. How many of us call ourselves stupid when we make a mistake? Simply saying "I made a mistake" is much more kind and is free of judgment.

Awareness of our judging nature provides us an opportunity to accept this behavior and take action to improve ourselves. My awareness of when I am judgmental is growing. I catch myself finding dandelions and when I do, I remember the beauty of the flower instead of the label of the weed.

An opportunity to suspend judgment came many months later. Christmas evening, my family was lingering at the dinner table after a wonderful holiday feast. We were cocooned in a rosy glow of togetherness that comes only once a year when our far flung members come home. Someone knocked at the door. When I answered, it was stranger looking for a man who used to live on the street. He told me he did odd jobs for this man and was looking for work. He apologized repeatedly for disturbing me yet we continued to talk. He was homeless having used his allotted thirty days at the shelter. He would not qualify for another shelter until the next day. He was wearing a new red coat and bright blue shoes he received at the shelter as a Christmas gift. He insisted on showing me his identification card as if to prove he counted in this world. He asked for work and I had none. It was night, my yard was free from leaves and there was no snow to shovel. My long absence concerned my son. When he saw the man, my son's posture stiffened and I told him I was all right. I prepared a bag of oranges and Christmas cookies. I gave him the bag and ten dollars, the going rate for one night stay in the hotel next to the shelter. He thanked me and apologizing all the while, he left.

Back at the dinner table, my family discussed the pros and cons of giving handouts to people. "Is it a handout or is it help?" I asked. It was Christmas, and I remembered the dandelion and judgments. Was he a dandelion or an opportunity to serve the God within?

> *"Whoever welcomes this little child in my name welcomes*
> *me; and whoever welcomes me welcomes the one who sent me."*

—Luke 9:48. NPV, 2002

Later, the New Year was six days old and several inches of dry fluffy snow arrived. The homeless man returned to our door. He reminded my son that I had helped him on Christmas night and he was here to return the favor. He shoveled the snow from our steps and walks. And thanked my son several times for the help he received Christmas night.

Dandelions are also inside of us. In proverbs, divine wisdom gives a dinner party. We need to invite all aspects of ourselves to the table for nourishment. It is easy to nourish and accept our loving and generous selves. For our divine wisdom, we need to also integrate the confused or wandering parts of ourselves; our mourning parts for relationships and dreams lost or not met; all parts we label not acceptable or weeds. By allowing our dandelion aspects to unite with us, we strengthen our I AM presence. Our I AM presence connects with God's I AM or I CAN, the power and energy of creation. Through this connection to God and the power of creation, we can co-create our reality.

THE DANDELION'S PRAYER

Dear Holy Presence, please be with me now and forevermore. Guide my thoughts, words and actions to honor the divine in me and in others. Help me remember that in honoring all others and myself, I honor you. I AM creating, in the fullness of my capacity, love as your Divine intention conceived it to be. And so it is. Thank you God.

4

THE LAVENDER

May 2003. I was unsure what was happening to me. I could feel waves of energy washing over me and sometimes so forcefully, I felt off balance. The energy was especially strong in the garden. Yet at times it happened at work. I am a registered nurse and worked in an academic medical center. Seeing and hearing Nature Spirits was beyond the scientific realm of healthcare. How could I tell my friends, also nurses, who were grounded in science? What would they think? As much as I wanted support, I decided to keep my experiences with Nature separate from my professional life. I began living with this secret.

I could not get Edward out of my mind. I drew him with the intention that onto the paper he would be out of my mind and I would be relieved of what was happening to me. The colored pencils quickly moved across the paper and the image of Edward and a hosta emerged. I smiled remembering our conversation. He said he had waited a long time for me and his to do list proved it. The drawing complete, I walked through the house and immediately received another picture. It was as if I had a large screen in my brain on which images flashed. The image was three-dimensional and so real I could not be sure if it was in my mind's eye or right before me. He was a small male, with large ears and hands, dressed in blue tails complete with a top hat.

I wondered out loud. "How many are there?"

"We are a community. I am Robert, the Lavender."

That evening I drew Robert. He looked younger than Edward. Thin and small, wispy as a lavender's stem with strawberry blonde hair and large ears protruding from under his blue top hat. He had round rosy red cheeks and a clean shaven face. His blue tailcoat and trousers gave him a gentlemanly appearance. I could not imagine Robert running barefoot under the hostas like Edward.

The lavender lived in a large flowerpot on the deck. I loved lavender. The climate and the garden's exposure did not suit lavender. However, a pot on the deck could manage nicely. I often ran my fingers through the stems and inhaled the gentle fragrance. Lavender soothes and brings calm. I felt the jostling of life. I took a quick inventory of life's demands, work, long hours, short deadlines, multiple projects, hundreds of email and voicemail messages, caring for a family, cooking, cleaning, laundry, errands, the dogs, traffic, phones, pagers and countless people needing and wanting something. I wondered where the list ends. Where do I fit? Am I at the top of the list or the bottom?

"You are often at the bottom. You give yourself away."

"Sometimes I choose to put other things first." As soon as I said that, I knew even I did not believe it. Too noble. The truth is, it is easier to say yes than no. The result of too many yeses is not caring for myself.

"An excuse!" Robert put his hands on his hips for emphasis. "How often do you really make that an aware and conscious choice? And now think about when you are unaware and therefore not able to make a choice. What happens to your sense of calm?" He dropped his hands to his side and stood patiently waiting for an answer.

"I begin to feel I am doing everything and I can't do what I want. I can feel my stomach churn. Resentment I suppose." Another character building, soul lesson was taking place. Why can't we talk about something light, fairies or sunbeams perhaps?

"You are not choosing to do what you want. You always have a choice. Are you joyfully engaged in your duties? I think not. I hear your sighs. I can feel when your work is motion only with no heart or joy. And I have seen you at times complete the same work filled with love and peace, lost in the flow of time. You create two intentions for the same assignment and two different feelings will result. Again this is your choice. And this is your lesson."

"But time." Another great excuse. This one I keep handy and use it often. Perhaps it would even work with a Nature Being. It was becoming clear to me that I could not choose the lesson or the place and time. What if I am busy? Oh no, what if they come to work with me? What if they come to work with me and want to talk?

"Humans are so focused on time! There is plenty of time. Do not use time as the excuse for not caring for you. It takes no time to be on the top of your list. You are here for a purpose. Your purpose must be fulfilled. Place yourself first and you will discover there is plenty of time for you, your divine purpose and everything you desire to accomplish. When you forget to choose and you will, remember the lavender, feel the soothing calm flow into you. And then in your awareness make the choice. This is a lesson you must learn. Until you master it, you will continue to create dramas that present the opportunity to place yourself first."

"Dramas?" I like taking credit for the good times, good feelings and good results. But dramas sound like messes. Messes just happen. I wanted no responsibility for messes. Can I look at a mess and say with pride I created that? In a mess is there any choice? A dramatic mess would be if Edward or who knows what comes to work with me and talks. I can picture Edward hovering over my desk, tapping his foot on what I don't know, since he seems to float, while my boss comes in to discuss something vitally important. That would be a drama. I decide that would be Edward's responsibility, not mine. If I don't want it why would I create it?

"Yes, your life theater will present to you situations where you have the chance to place your needs first so you can be fulfilled. If you do not choose to place yourself at the top of your list in that situation, then another situation will occur to offer you another opportunity to learn. You are responsible for your choices. All of your choices. Anticipate these dramas will escalate until you accept the learning. There is pure peace and calm in living your divine purpose instead of focusing on the resentment you create by not doing what you want. It is all your choice and your creation of reality."

THE LAVENDER'S PRAYER

Dearest Divine One! Awaken within me my divine purpose. Set me on this journey. For I now know my purpose is not a destination but a journey. Help me relinquish my human need for control. My safety was never in my control. Embrace me with the safety of peace as I joyfully choose to follow my divine purpose with all of my beingness. I AM walking my divine path in the fullness of God, one step at a time. And so it is. Thank you God.

5

SAYING YES

July 2003. Edward's hosta home, one of the chartreuse giant hostas, was blooming. I sat near it.

I focused on the large white blossom of Edward's hosta. The hosta was surrounded by a light purple aura. The aura wasn't constant but a motion of waves, wide then narrow around the plant. I knew from gardening, the roots of the hosta are very strong in a large centered clump. I continued to focus and felt myself merge with the hosta. Many stems arose from the plant. Each stem supported one large leaf. I felt the hosta's energy compress through the narrowness of the stem and burst wide and free in the leaf. The center leaves formed a whorl upward to the sky. The outer leaves formed a canopy over the ground creating shelter. I became very small. Looking upward I could see the sky's brightness shine through the leaf. I stood under the leaves, hidden in the cover, feeling their protection. A tall stem, taller than the leaves, came from the plant's center and supported the blossoms.

The essence of the hosta is divine protection and connection. Grounded in the earth, reaching for the sky and blooming for the heavens is the hosta's lesson.

"We are here for you. We delight in your growth. The Spirit works through you. The Hostas are your first connection. Send love to us."

"Edward are you there?" I looked around the hostas hoping to see him. I felt safe with Edward. Not knowing who/what might pop up next unnerved me.

"Yes I am here. You can listen to the plants without me. Yet I am here."

"I am not sure about all of this," I said waving my hand to indicate the garden.

"These experiences excite and scare me. I'd like to feel a happy wonder about what will happen next but I am too scared."

"I will guide you. If you prefer, I will speak to you on behalf of the plants. The bloom says reach for heaven by focusing your energy here. The bloom is your potential. It is you reflecting God's beauty and love."

My first step was complete. I was living my commitment to Nature. I gardened cooperatively with Nature and followed Nature's instructions. Imperfectly. Sometimes I pulled a weed and afterwards remembered I first should have asked it to leave and given it time to do so. Sometimes I resisted the message or lesson. At times, my humanness and the personality of the ego impaired my ability to act on my commitment to Nature. Yet I remained committed. It was an imperfect, fully human commitment. My faith was stronger but I frequently still asked why and how. I knew with faith these questions were unnecessary. I was slowly beginning to replace the demand to know with a curiosity of what is next.

6

THE LOVING TREE

23

My second step was saying yes unconditionally. Yes to Universal Love. Yes to Universal Healing. Saying yes reconnected me to the knowledge that I am one with God and aligned myself with the greater spiritual reality. Nature continued to speak to me and the messages were of Faith, Grace and Gratitude.

July 2003. I leaned over the deck railing and looked down on a small triangular bed of dark green hostas and shiny ground cover. The honeysuckle vine was thick with leaves and its flowers were beginning to fade in the summer heat. This bed once had a large locust tree with extensive roots traveling across the ground. Large black tumor-like growths had covered the tree's trunk hinting at the extensive disease inside. A team of men with screaming chain saws removed the tree. The stump remained, covered by ground cover and hosta leaves. Planting anything in that area would be a challenge due to the tree roots and only very small holes could be dug for equally small plants. The deck, an outdoor living room, looked over all the beds in the garden. I loved to sit outdoors and enjoy the view. A tree in that bed would filter the setting sun. I knew the old stump would have to be removed to dig a hole large enough to plant a tree. As I leaned over the deck railing and looked down on the bed, I wished out loud for a tree in that spot.

A few weeks later, I was again looking down on the bed and I saw a small maple seedling.

"My tree! You came. I wished for a tree and you came!"

I was so excited. I wished for a tree and got one. I called my friend to come and see. "I have a tree."

"Where?" his tone doubtful.

"Right there. See?" I ran down the steps and pointed to a small six-inch-tall seedling. "Right there. See? It is perfect. It will shade the deck and filter the afternoon sun."

"You'll be an old lady before it is big enough to offer shade. If you want a tree so much, let's buy a big one. A proper tree from the nursery."

I refused to listen. "It is perfect. It will grow fast." I turned and faced the tree. Cupping one of the tiny leaves in my hands, "I love you tree."

"Edward, it is a tree. Just what I wished. Can you see this wonderful tree?"

"The tree says 'I AM love.' Shhh. Listen and you can hear the tree for yourself. Still your mind and open your heart and listen." "I AM love."

The tree did grow fast. By fall it was over twelve feet tall. Thin green branches leaned over the deck and cradled the spot where I usually sat. I loved sitting with my back to the tree and the branches hugging me. I felt the tree's love. The tree had a serene light sea blue-green aura. The tree spoke few words. And I, feeling more secure, initiated all of our conversations.

"I love you tree." "I AM love."

Autumn came. In October, I put the garden to bed. The maple trees in the park up the street turned bright orange and yellow. My neighbor's maple tree was also bright yellow. My tree was green. It must be warmer in that spot I told myself, a microclimate feeling like summer to the tree. The tree remained green. November came. It was cold. Everywhere I looked, the maple trees had lost their leaves. In fact all the trees had lost their leaves. My tree was green with no hint of changing color or dropping any leaves. A week before Thanksgiving, the weatherman predicted the next week would bring our first hard freeze of the season.

"Edward, a hard freeze will kill this tree. It is not ready. Why hasn't it followed the rule of Autumn? What should I do?" I was anxious for an answer.

"You already know."

"Edward if I knew, I'd do it. I am asking for your help." I thought it was so apparent I did not know what to do about this tree that I shouldn't even have to ask.

"My help is that you already know the answer. Be still. When I instruct you to be still I am speaking of your mind. The answer is not in your mind. Answers always lie in the heart."

I repeated, "Be still, open my heart." I sat down and closed my eyes. "What can I do to help this tree prepare for winter?" The question posed, I began to meditate. Sometime later, I opened my eyes. I knew.

"I love you tree."

"I AM love."

"I know you love me. I think you don't want to go to sleep and leave me. You must. A hard freeze will be coming and winter too. If you are not asleep, the freeze will kill you. Please go to sleep. I will be here. I will watch over you. Even in winter I sit outdoors. I will sit by you while you sleep. And I will be here next spring when you wake up. We will be together. I love you. Please go to sleep. I will be here when you wake up."

"I AM love."

In one week's time the tree turned yellow and dropped its leaves. The hard freeze hit just as predicted and winter came. The tree slept.

March 2004, the tree's buds were very tiny, tight and dark red. I watched them slowly grow and finally a tiny leaf tip emerged from one of the buds.

"Hello tree. Welcome to Spring! I love you."

"I AM love."

The leaves grew and the tree grew. It was as tall as the second story on the house.

June 2004 a cool summer evening was perfect for a dinner on the deck by the tree. As we ate, I looked at the tree. I noticed a large leaf on an upper branch. It was huge.

"Have you ever seen a leaf that big?" I asked pointing.

It was the size of a dinner plate. The more I looked, the more I found. The usual normal sized maple leaves were mere infants growing into their full gigantic splendor. Almost everyday, I thought to myself, I have never seen a leaf that big. Most measured sixteen inches across. I asked the tree permission to harvest a few. I coated them in silver leaf and framed them to always enjoy the tree's gift of big leaves.

Autumn 2004 and the tree was turning yellow right on schedule with all the other maple trees in the neighborhood. The tree was now too wide for its position next to the garage and house. I knew it would have to be trimmed.

"I love you tree."

"I AM love."

"Tree, you are too big to be so close to the buildings. When you go to sleep, I will have you trimmed. I will wait till you are asleep so you won't feel any pain from the trimming. And I will make certain the trimmer respects you and treats you with care. You will be trimmed to that fork in your trunk." I said pointing. "I am sorry to have you trimmed. It is the only way to protect you and the buildings. If you get too big you wouldn't be able to stay. And I love you so."

It was so difficult for me to even discuss trimming. I could feel tears welling up in my eyes. Could the tree's full potential be expressed if it is trimmed? The leaves dropped and the tree was bare. Time to find a trimmer. November brought a thunderstorm. It was a big storm. Jagged streaks of lightening crossed the sky and claps of thunder boomed. I stood at the back door, watching the storm and listening for the tornado sirens. It was dark. Only when lightening flashed could I see the tree or the garden. The winds picked up and the tree swayed wildly. I saw only bits of the movement but knew the tree could not bend much more in the wind. I heard a crack. My heart jumped but in the dark I could not see what happened. Perhaps it was the old tree in the neighbor's yard breaking or a branch falling. Lightening flashed and I saw it was my tree that cracked. It had broken in the force of the wind. Soon the thunder and lightening ceased and only a gentle drizzle remained. Standing in the rain, I inspected the tree. The tree had snapped at the fork, the very spot where it was to be trimmed.

"Oh tree. You pruned yourself." I felt sick inside. The sight of the broken tree knotted my stomach and wrenched my heart.

"I AM love."

"You trimmed to spare me. I love you tree."

"I AM love."

Love is the creative force in the Universe. Love precedes all creation. Love forms the energy which becomes matter on the physical plane. Love can create a tree. Love can manifest miracles.

THE LOVING TREE'S PRAYER

Most beautiful Mother Earth who is at one with God, thank you for the beauty of your presence, dressed and decorated by Nature. I see God's love in the beauty of your waters, flowers and trees. Still my mind and open my heart to the complete expression of love. Through love, I AM creating that which I wish to be. I AM love. And so it is. Thank you Mother Earth. Thank you God.

7

THE WILD SPACE

Returning to August 2003. I was in the garden sweeping up dead leaves and I felt a sudden urge to fence off a triangular section of the garden for a wild space. It was a small bed, eight feet on each side, bounded by the garage and the fence along the property line. It contained a honeysuckle vine, small dark green hostas and lots of ground cover. In creating the wild space, I committed to protect it from the intrusion of dogs and humans. I would not enter the space except for putting the garden to bed in the fall and preparing it for spring. I also promised the garden I would give notice when I needed to enter.

I sat in the garden, meditating, up popped Miss Sally, the Sweet Woodruff. She had gray hair in a tangle of curls. A purple and red hat defied gravity and sat on the side of her head. She wore a long skirt in assorted browns that could not hide her plump hips. She wrapped herself in an orange shawl. Nothing in her outfit matched. Her perpetual smile crinkled her eyes into narrow slits.

"Good afternoon, what is your name?"

"Miss Sally. You may address me as Miss Sally." Her head quivered slightly and matched the tremble in her voice. "Thank you for the wild space. It is good. Your receptivity to our energy and suggestions has grown. You are a more sensitive listener."

"That urge to create the wild space came from you?" I hoped any future suggestions would consider my schedule, other to do lists and my energy or fatigue. I did not want to be up in the middle of the night following an urge that actually came from Nature.

"Yes. To ease your human understanding, I'll say yes the suggestion to create came from me. It is energy flowing through you. You were an instrument of Nature to create the wild space. You did very well." Her head bobbed up and down while she spoke and her hat held fast.

"Focus this week on the garden's energies. You feel the vibrations. Sit and learn what they feel like so you can detect shifts in the energy. You are now learning rapidly and must integrate all this knowledge into your work. The garden is but a tool to connect with other energies and the universal spirit. There will be other guides along your path. You will recognize their presence through the vibrations of their energy. We reveal ourselves in perfect time as there is only but perfection and there is no time. A continuum of spirit is what is. We are a part of you and you are a part of us. All is one."

The energy usually came over my body in waves. How I would detect differences in the energy when I perceived it as one large wave?

Edward spoke a few days later while I sat in the garden. "The garden is sacred space. Your place is feeling the heartbeat of the earth. Stay in tune with the Nature Spirits. Call forth to the spirits for their ancient experience. They are your guides. This sacred space is grounded by your care for the earth and all living beings. Your intention is all. You find answers to love and harmony by working in cooperation with the Universe to protect the planet Earth. Say yes to loving all. Do not question if the love is deserved. Love all. Loving all is healing. Power is the act of loving."

8

THE LILAC

September 2003. I was in Ohio visiting my mother. Her kitchen window overlooked a large grassy yard ringed by an overflowing garden crowded with plants and a small fishpond. Ancient lilacs and black walnut trees were the backdrop for the pond.

As I looked out the window, I heard a lilac calling me. "Old man not now. I am busy visiting my mom. I promise I will talk to you later."

My response was so automatic; it took me a while to realize Nature outside of my own garden was talking to me. Intermittently, I heard and felt the lilac calling me. My mother and I were busy talking, shopping, eating and laughing. I forgot the lilac in the distraction of the activities.

When I finally remembered to visit the lilac, I stood before it holding a heart shaped leaf in each hand imagining the delicious scent of its spring flowers. I felt it trying to reach me. Yet I was unable to discern what it wanted to tell me. I was too distracted to still my mind and listen as Edward had instructed me so many times.

"Old man I can feel you calling me. Yet I don't know what you want. I am going to take a picture of you. When I return home and can peacefully meditate I will connect with you. Perhaps in the quiet, looking at your picture, I will be able to receive your message." I gave it some coffee grounds as a small gesture of my love.

October 2003. A lazy weekend afternoon and I was in a dozy, drowsy state after meditating. The Old man spoke.

THE OLD MAN AND THE LILAC

She heard me calling
She felt me wash over her
She even took my picture
She does not know my name.
I am the Sentinel.
I stand over time.
My boughs offer refuge
My heart is in every leaf.
She sees me as the old man.
I have no beginning and no end.
Tell her I am no different than she.
She and I belong to the Universe
Where there is no time.

I find there is no time when living fully in the perfection of each moment without attachment to the outcome.

"When I am immersed in the joy of the present moment, time stands still." I said out loud to no one as I stretched out on the bed.

"Time standing still is a human illusion because there is no time. Humans created linear time to organize their lives. In the moment, connected to the Universe, time is not linear." Edward stretched his arms wide and tapped his foot for emphasis. I thought I was alone. Alone on my bed. He better not pop up in the bathroom. I sat up.

"But I have felt time stand still. When I feel lost in time, I get so much done."

"Time is an illusion. It cannot stand still. That would mean a pause from moment to moment. Impossible because only this moment exists. The next moment is in the future and does not exist. Humans created the illusion of the past and future so you can plan and function in the physical world. There is no past or future. Only now. Linear time is not real. Time is limitless. When you feel time standing still, you really are experiencing the connection to the Universe in the moment of now."

"Edward I have felt the limitless of time. Time is limitless." I was excited this made sense to me. I am amazed what I accomplish in that space. In the present moment and connected to the Universe, anything can be accomplished with the blink of an eye. It feels so wonderful to be connected to the flow of the universal creative mind and energy. Then my busy mind starts chattering and I step out of the universal flow. The connection is lost. As soon as we think about the past or the future we have moved out of the right now. All we have is right now. Only now this moment is here and is perfect.

Edward smiled, "Creation is in the now where there is no time." He raised his hands above his head, clasped them together as if in prayer and slowly brought them down to his chest. His hands rested over his heart. I thought he must be thanking God that I grasped this lesson.

THE LILAC'S PRAYER

Oh most Holy Father-Mother God, how great thou art! As May brings the Lilac into full bloom and perfumes the world to remind us of its transformation, bring to our minds the present. Open our hearts so we sense and perceive the transformation of humanity. As we perceive what is possible, open our vision so that we see from the whole and are not limited by our own viewpoint. Guide us in this vision to create the will to transform ourselves into the most holy images of God. And as the new seeks to emerge, grant us courage to embody and live our presence now. And so it is. Thank you God.

9
COMPOST

Autumn 2003, I finished building the raised garden bed shaped like an arrow per Edward's instructions.

"You need to fill this bed with compost that you have made." Edward was standing in the empty bed trying to wiggle his toes into the hard dirt.

"What compost? I haven't made any compost. I don't know how to do that." Nothing like an immediate negative response. No thought or consideration. Just No. As soon as I spoke, I remembered my commitment to say yes and act in faith.

"OK. I am saying yes and I don't know what to do. I am relying on your instructions to create this stuff. You will give me directions? Oh and I don't want the dogs getting into the compost so tell me how to handle that."

"We will guide you in the making of the compost. The compost will strengthen and balance the land."

By some means that I cannot explain, my mind flashed a picture of an organic composting supply store outside the city in a neighborhood I didn't frequent. I remembered Miss Sally and the wild space. Perhaps this was another example of a Nature Being sending me instructions energetically. Due to its narrow market niche, I had never visited the store. There, I purchased a black round compost container. I liked the idea of spinning the drum. The only thing I knew about compost was that it required turning. I deliberately read nothing about composting. Faith in Nature would lead the composting activities. For the first time I did not feel so bad when I found a bag of spoiled lettuce long forgotten in the refrigerator. I simply put it in the composter and was grateful the energy would be recycled into the garden instead of the trash bin. One day I took kitchen scraps out to the composter and saw a three-dimensional triangular shaped clod of dirt surrounded by yellow light. The triangular shape was both his head and body. He had skinny arms and legs with knobby knees extending from this clod-like body. He was wearing oversized mitts and boots. His out of proportion fashion accessories and odd shaped body created a comical figure.

I suppressed a laugh. "Hello. Are you in charge of the soil?" I asked feeling very proud that this time I was not frightened or surprised to be seeing a Nature Spirit.

"No. I'm Chuck. The compost caretaker." "You look like dirt to me."

"Compost. I'm in compost. I'm wearing boots aren't I?" "Yes."

"Compost. Just chuck it in here baby."

"Oh Edward, 'chuck it in here', what a corny joke."

"He is wearing red boots. We honor your sense of humor" he smiled as if quite pleased with himself.

I followed Chuck's cryptic instructions. Sometimes he told me to add water and brown leaves. He would tell me when to stop adding to the pile and how long it needed to rest. I spread the compost when and where he directed. The first batch of compost was spread on the arrow of life garden bed. This bed rested over the winter.

As my last garden task that fall, I planted a juniper. Now all of the instructions Edward had given to me were complete. The small conical shrub was placed at the end of a bed teeming with a variety of giant hostas. Next to the juniper, I placed the fairy shelter also constructed following Edward's design.

10
THE JUNIPER

A few weeks later Jenniperleah, the juniper, spoke. "I am silvery light like the juniper berry. The juniper is settling in well. The silver blues and greens are a good backdrop for the yellows and chartreuses of the hostas. They are so loud. We are cool, restful and serene." Her breath lingered on the word serene as if she breathed the word instead of speaking.

"I haven't thought of the hostas as loud."

"There are so many and they are large and bright, grabbing attention and space. The one you call Edward has been directing energies in the garden. It is he that brought me here." She turned away from the hostas, leaned forward and whispered, "Edward recognizes the importance of my gift."

"The juniper has a gift?" I whispered in reply.

"Yes. We all do. Each of us brings unique gifts to you for a blessed healing. These are your lessons in connecting to the Source. Each of us brings an offering to assist you in this connection. I offer protection for your inner vision so you can see the lessons along your path. My message is for you to pay attention to your vision and complete your lessons. Clear your pathway. Run your hands through my branches and collect the scent." She vanished in a thin silver wisp of breath.

THE JUNIPER'S PRAYER

I AM calling forth to my Guardian Angel, the loving one assisting me with my journey. Help me recognize that events and experiences occur in my life in perfect order, each serving as the foundation for the next. Help me release judgment in this process, remembering it does not serve me to compare my path to another's. Rest my curious mind with the peace that my journey will unfold in its natural way. Tune my listening so that instead of trying to direct my path, I may hear directions while on my path. Open my eyes to see the miracles in the synchronicity of events. Expand my heart's delight with this journey. And so it is. Thank you God.

11

THE CHRISTMAS ROSE

December 2003. It was cold. Snow flurries marked several December days. The garden was quiet. I engaged in the bustle of the holidays. One afternoon, I stood outside on the deck and looked at the sky. It was pure white, a snow sky. The flakes were just beginning to fall and I delighted in the holiday atmosphere of the falling snow. As I watched the tiny flakes, I glimpsed a spot of color in the garden. It was startling to see color in a bare and sleeping garden. One of the rose bushes had a pink bud on it. How could the rose bloom after weeks of frost and hard freezes? Not trusting my sight, I photographed it hoping the photograph would show me what was real. Over the week the bud opened and displayed a full pink, perfect rose blossom. Everyone who saw it shared in my astonishment.

"Thank you Rose for this beautiful blossom. Your pinkness is so gentle and yet so bright in the bare garden." I now believed the blossom was real. "We are the gift of the Angels. This season, we bring the tidings of joy. Feel the joy and allow yourself to emerge into the fullness of your perfection. As you did not expect this blossom, look for joy when you least expect it."

"Edward, I am calling you. Isn't this rose fabulous? Are you and the Nature Beings enjoying this rose too?"

"All is divine and joy is found in all. Go to the depths of your experiences. Even where you see pain, there is love. And in love there is joy. The unfolding of this blossom is your unfolding to become that which you have committed. Take joy in this journey." Edward added a sprig of juniper to his lime green shirt. He smiled at his holiday accessory.

THE CHRISTMAS ROSE'S PRAYER

Dearest Holy Infant please hear my prayer as my heart sends it upward to the heavens on tiny pink rose petals wrapped in the blessing of peace. Thank you for joy which softens the harshness of winter. Please bestow a blessing on each being walking this earth that all will know peace. Open every heart so that all may become creators of peace. May we master this art on earth as it is in the heavens. Keep me mindful of cherishing peace in the joy of this life. And so it is. Thank you God.

12

THE MOONFLOWER

January 2004. As winter's cold breath crept under the door and rattled the windows, I was lost in the spring and summer flowers found in gardening catalogs. I dreamt of filling the arrow of life bed with roses, pink, salmon and white. With careful attention to watering and feeding, I decided the bed could support four rose bushes. I envisioned Alyssum filling the borders with delicate tiny flowers. I pushed to the very back of my mind, my agreement with Nature. I did not think about gardening in cooperation with Nature. I was not interested in Nature's plan; I was too excited about my plan for roses.

"No." I knew the 'no' came from Edward. I felt his presence before I heard his distinctive voice.

"No? Edward, no what?" I asked as if I didn't know it was about the roses.

"No to roses."

"This bed is perfect for roses. It is narrow and raised and has natural protection from freezing. And I love roses." I hoped my positive tone strengthened my argument.

"This bed is not for roses." "But why?"

"Dear one, still yourself. Listen to Nature's love flowing in and out of your heart."

"But."

"Shh. Still. Quiet your voice. Permit Nature's love to flow through you. Open your heart. Listen."

"I hear you. I am only listening to you Edward." I said with a poutful tone any four-year-old would envy. "I can't hear anyone else. Nature has not said no. Only you have said no." Continuing with four-year-old tactics, I tried a divide and conquer approach, pitting Nature against Edward.

"Shh. Still. You are resisting the message as you stubbornly cling to a plan you created without Nature. You cannot make an intermittent contract. You cannot step off your path when it suits you. Do not ignore your purpose. This is about your life and the earth. All is one. What you would do within the garden bed so is done to your life and the earth. Your intention to one is mirrored as your intention to all. Presently be still and listen. This is the choice you made."

Spring 2004. I did not hear Nature present a plan for the arrow of life garden. All seemed very quiet. Perhaps my desire to plant roses blocked my ability to hear Nature. I suspected Edward spoke for Nature. My wish for roses was strong enough that I needed to hear an answer from another voice. Maybe I was simply stubborn and resistant. It was spring and time to plant. I went to the garden nursery, wandered around hoping Nature would speak to me there.

At the store, I walked up and down the rows of plants. Nothing. No voice. I stopped by begonias. Nothing. I stopped by ornamental grasses. Nothing. Marigolds and no voice. The roses tempted me. Nature hadn't spoken to me. Perhaps Nature changed her mind and roses were permissible. I touched a leaf.

"No."

I heard that. I thought for a split second about pretending I didn't hear it. The No was clear and impossible to ignore. I continued to wander and stop by plants. Nature did not speak. I walked past a seed display. I heard lots of whispering. It was difficult to discern what was being said. As I approached the seeds everyone talked at once.

"Here we are. Right here. Here we are! Look at us."

"Seeds?"

"Yes. Of course."

I stood before the seed display. So many choices. In reality there were many seeds promising a variety of plants and flowers but only two choices were given by Nature. Moonflower was the first choice. Coreopsis was the second choice. I had never grown moonflowers and I welcomed them to my garden. Coreopsis was fine in other people's gardens. I didn't want it in mine. I stubbornly clung to my wish for roses, not coreopsis.

I planted the moonflower seeds first. As I tucked each seed under a blanket of soil, I marked the spot with a twig. In the past, I have pulled up the very seeds I planted. Desired seedlings and weed seedlings look very similar. Twigs marking the seed spots prevent weeding mishaps. Further down the bed, about two feet, I planted the coreopsis seeds and marked the spots with twigs. The moonflowers came up first and were large seedlings. They grew very fast and quickly needed a trellis on which to climb.

"I am the Moonflower and my lesson is authenticity. There is healing in being authentic. Living your truth provides you with power. In your truth and power you will find freedom. Healing is bringing your spirit to peace. All matter comes from energy. A spirit at peace is not forming energy leading to disease. Living authentically leads to ease."

"How do you live authentically?"

"I create luminous white flowers. Each blossom unfolds in her glory for only one night and when the sun rises, the blossom closes forever. Most will never see my beauty in the darkness of the night. Yet I still bloom. I create magnificent bright flowers with a delicate scent because that is my true self. The blooms do not change in size or beauty to suit a viewer or to gain approval. That is authenticity. Creating glorious glowing flowers is my divine destiny and my bliss. I am at ease with my spirit as I keep to my divine destiny. I am ease. I am authentic."

THE MOONFLOWER'S PRAYER

To the angels and heavenly hosts whom I love in the truth, I call for your assistance. If I have lost my true self; help me reconnect. If I have forgotten my true self; remind me. If I cannot see my true self; show me. Ignite in me a passion for living my truth in every way, everyday. As my passion grows, my spirit is at peace. I AM living authentically as my true self, a divine spark from God. And so it is. Thank you God.

13

THE
COREOPSIS

The coreopsis came up next to the twigs and also began to vine. I thought it was odd the coreopsis was vining but I hadn't saved the seed packets to check. There are many different coreopsis varieties; I decided I purchased a variety that vined. The moonflower grew over the trellis and up the side of the house. The coreopsis vines grew over the side of the bed and down the garden walk. I lifted and moved them like ropes when I swept the walk. I continued to think they were odd. Nature told me to plant coreopsis and I did. They sprouted by the twigs and they were blooming yellow flowers just like coreopsis. Therefore the vines were coreopsis.

The coreopsis continued to grow down the garden walk the summer of 2004. The vines were covered with yellow flowers with a slight orange blush. One day I picked up the vines to move them and spotted a small round tan ball near the side of the garden bed. It was a cantaloupe the size of a soft ball. This was not coreopsis, it was cantaloupe!

"I am your creation."

"No, you aren't really. I didn't plant you. For me, impossible. I didn't do anything."

"You say you are unaware that you created me? True you didn't buy a packet of cantaloupe seeds and plant them. However, you were just as deliberate in creating me."

"I am still sure I didn't do anything to create you. You have appeared here all by yourself."

"It is curious and amusing how humans can be so surprised by their life events. You act as if it just happened. Can you see the connection of your thoughts to my appearance? You did not want coreopsis. Your thoughts are the start of creation and your feelings give a vibration. When the vibration of your feelings and the thought match, creation takes form. What you think, you attract. All things form first in vibration, then form in the physical realm."

"No. I don't think I wished for cantaloupe. Edward where are you? I am talking to an interloping cantaloupe."

"'I didn't do that'", you said. 'That is not what I would have wanted to happen', you said. Denial of responsibility. You were surprised to see me sprout in the garden. 'I didn't plant cantaloupe', you said. How long did you deny I was a cantaloupe? The blossoms, the vines? Coreopsis? I heard you say that looks like a melon blossom but not grasp your role in the creation. Not until you stood face to face with the melon growing on the vine did you acknowledge the reality of my presence."

The cantaloupe's tone was belligerent. Perhaps it was difficult to lie on the brick garden walk in the hot sun completely unseen and ignored. No life on soft soil in a special melon bed carefully tended and wanted. Poor melon.

The cantaloupe's annoyance with me was unmistakable. I stepped back, lest a vine should wrap itself around my ankles. Thinking it best to avoid an assault from a cantankerous cantaloupe, I called out "Edward, Edward, Edward, be here now!"

"The vines, blossoms and melons were manifested through your creation. This garden corresponds to the landscape of the thinker, you. All that you experience is your creation." Edward stepped in between the vines and stood on top of the cantaloupe. I waved my hand to signal him to move. Why add to the cantaloupe's irritation by standing on him? Edward ignored my signals and remained balanced on the melon.

"I am pretty sure I didn't create him. Right now I can't say abracadabra and have a cantaloupe growing."

"Actually creation can be that fast. The Universe does not have to obey human laws of science. All-That-Is, another name for the great Universe, is the source of all energy and creation. When you experience your reality as All-That-Is, then All-That-Is becomes your reality. The universal energy flows through you to manifest your creation. Your soul's journey is a journey in creation. Rest in the perfection of the moment knowing it is as it should be." Edward hopped from the cantaloupe to the soil and wiggled his toes burying them in the dirt. "Ahhh." I think the cantaloupe sighed too.

"If I create my reality, why am I creating re-runs? The same thing over and over. Why?"

"Everything leads back to Source. It is law. Circle of nature. Is the lesson a repeat? Don't fret. I hear you ask when I am ever going to get this. Understanding sometimes arrives in small parcels. You are growing at perfect speed just like the garden. You will arrive at divine oneness with the great Universe exactly when it is your time. Take joy in the lessons you have chosen and created. Don't compare your lessons with others'. At the perfect moment, all will arrive in oneness with the Universe. Remember the seasons of the garden. New life in the spring, blossoms in the summer, fruits of the harvest in autumn and rest in the winter. The circle of completion always starting and ending with God or Source. So follows your life experiences. New ones arriving as others diminish in completion. Do not mourn their passing. Whisper gratitude in the farewell. The lesson and the people who play a role in your lesson are a gift. A gift of service, the fruit of energy. And you are forever changed by it. Be grateful for this fruit that nourishes you. Whenever you become upset and wonder how or why something happened to you, stop, and instead be curious. I wonder why I created this and what I will learn from it. What is the cantaloupe, the fruit of possibility, for me?"

THE CANTALOUPE'S PRAYER

Father, Father, Father, be with me now. You have said everything is possible for he who believes. Seal this truth in my heart of hearts. Connect my heart to my mind so that I may know this always. Awaken my mind and my heart should I ever question a possibility. Instill in me joyful imagination as I delight in the possibility of my life and the world. I AM dwelling in the sacred privilege of my possibilities and choices. And so it is. Thank you God.

14
THE DAY LILY

Summer 2004 continued. Yellow and orange day lilies line the back fence, decorating the cobblestone alley. They brightly face the sunshine, gently waving in the breeze. They are very hardy and handle the extreme conditions of the alley well. They withstand tromping by feet and survive only on rainfall. Each spring they surface before the days and nights are frost free and nonetheless are unaffected by the late spring freezes.

"I see the sun and feel its warmth."

"You have the same warm orange blaze as the sun." I looked around for the source of the voice and saw only the day lily's flower.

"I reflect the brightness of life and love in my being. Self worth comes from trusting the knowing of who we are. My stem holds many buds, each blooming one day at a time. Knowing there is always more you can let go of the future and rest your sight on the present. Gaze at my brightness and my beauty. This is all we really have, this moment and this blossom."

"Live my moment with all of my brightness?"

"Yes. The beauty of your presence is a reflection of your divine connection. There are gifts in every moment. Accept the gifts the Universe has to offer you. All you need is here now. There can be no worry because that is the future. There can be no regret because that is the past. Now. The divine is now. The divine is present. God is here now always."

THE DAY LILY'S PRAYER

Flowers of the heavenly hosts, salutations! Thank you for your beauty here on Earth. Open my heart to my highest presence. Assist me in knowing and trusting my true and real self. Remind me to revel in the beauty of my love and my gifts so that in my awe I may see their value to the world. I AM worthy of giving and receiving God's beautiful love. And so it is. Thank you God.

15

THE SEA

August 2004. In an ocean front cottage with my still sleeping family, I awoke early to write from my notes. Organized, I intended to follow a carefully planned outline. The ocean spoke.

"I am the sea."

Shocked, I didn't hear what else was said.

"I am writing only about lessons from my garden." I emphasized the word only.

"I am the sea."

"You are not on the outline. This is a story about lessons from my garden. How connecting to Nature is connecting to God." The outline was the plan. My plan. My goal to write two chapters during this beach vacation would only be achieved by holding to the outline.

"I am the sea."

"No. No. No. Prayer notes are next on my outline." I was committed to my outline, the plan. The ocean was not part of my garden or the outline. However, I did not want to miss the ocean's message. There would be time later to sort out the outline. I listened to the ocean.

"I am the sea. Oceans. Oh sense. Sensing. Smell the salt water. Feel its coolness. Taste the saltiness of the spray on your skin. Hear the roar of my waves crashing. See the waves rolling in one after another. I am the sea and I am constant. I never stop. I am always here. I will nourish your soul as I nourish the fish and the earth. I am white foam. I am green. I am blue and I am black. Yet I am. I envelop you with love. I am always here. I am constant."

THE SEA'S PRAYER

Neptune and all of the Universe's spirit guides of the sea strengthen my vigilance and resolve so I remain constant and faithful in my word. May my word, my promises, be as mighty as the sea whose presence is never questioned. As each promise kept washes over me in a wave of love, I AM fortified. And so it is. Thank you God.

16
THE WIND

Before I could take a breath and call Edward, I heard "I am the wind." Again I argued just as I had with the sea. I pointed out the outline and the plan. My need to control was evident. The argument does not need to be repeated here. I can assure you though, I argued for some time. I was not ready in my small human way to let go and accept the gift from Nature.

"I am the wind. I come from the four directions so I am one. What comes from the east eventually is the west. I bring change to what never was or ever is. Nothing remains the same. Many desire sameness. I want you to know that sameness is not constancy. The sea is constant but never the same. My winds bring change. A cool breeze on a warm day is welcome. A gentle wind to lift a kite adds play. I can also rip the roof off a house taking everything away. Is nothing left? Everything you need is left. Everything you are and need is inside you.

"Can you grow and change with a gentle breeze or will you need a tornadic wind? Can you hear the whisper of God or do you only listen to a roar? Do you react to the breeze like a kite, full of joy and color? Or do you resist until the wind must uproot your stubbornness? It is your choice how I will blow."

THE WIND'S PRAYER

Winds of God, breath of God, from whom all grace and good proceed, be with me now. I beseech thee to protect me from my human limitations. Preserve my devotion to you when I am distracted by earthly fixations. Strengthen me to stand and receive thy blessings so that I may change my human ways and magnify thy love and greatness forever. And so it is. Thank you God.

17

THE SEA GRASS

"Edward, Edward, Edward. Be here now!"

Nature Spirits work with a single plant species maintaining the plant in its specific form. Edward had introduced himself as a Nature Guardian and he moved freely about the garden. In fact, I first met him in my car. I suspected he was a Deva but never asked. Now I wished I knew the details of his responsibilities. His assistance with Nature was reassuring. How far could Edward roam? Did he only work with plants or could he help with elements like water and air?

"Edward where are you?" I walked outdoors and onto the beach. I turned away from the waves and faced east. The sky was a soft orange just above the mountain tops. I stood waiting for the magical flash of light when the sun's disk rose above the mountains.

Welcoming the sun and the official start of the day, I walked along the beach in wet sand where the last few inches of waves hurried in and out. The ocean water in the Pacific Northwest is cold, even in the summer. When my feet felt numb, I turned back and walked in the loose sand.

In front of our cottage, I sat in the sand and sifted it through my fingers. I was quiet and my mind still. "Hello dear one. Holiday retreat enjoyable?"

"Oh Edward. I am happy to see you." His toes like mine were wriggled under the sand. His pants were rolled up and his wispy hair moved in the breeze.

"I thought this was about the garden." I said waving vaguely at the cottage where the book notes laid. "And now the ocean and wind are talking. I took notes but they won't be a part of the story, will they? Maybe they didn't speak. Maybe it was my imagination. A dandelion is one thing, but the ocean? Really."

"Dear one be still."

"Edward you say that all the time. I need some help."

"Shh. Still. Be still. It is in the stillness of the now that it all happens." I started to open my mouth. "Shh. Be still now." he directed.

I exhaled and followed my breath in and out. I drew in a cord of golden light through the top of my head and out my feet, going deep into the center of the Earth. Grounded. Breath going in and out. In and out. In and out.

"You said yes unconditionally. Yes without limits. The garden walls offered security. Nature is the Universe. Dear one, your yes is as large as the Universe. Recall the Sentinel. You belong to the Universe."

"Where there is no time." I responded, completing the Sentinel's message. Slowly, I realized my purpose to help people connect to God through Nature was bigger than my outline. And since this came from God through Nature, I surrendered.

"Have you seen me? Every time you walk by, back and forth I wave."

Sea grass. I relaxed. Speaking to a plant was doable. A blade of grass is not as intimidating as the ocean or wind. Yes, I can sit here and talk to this sea grass all day.

"I like your long blades gently curling back toward the earth. How can you grow in just sand?" I smiled at the sea grass's enthusiastic energy.

"I flourish! Let your soul flourish. The human mistake is waiting for optimum conditions. The human excuse, 'it is not the right time'. There is no ideal soil. There is no perfect human time. The divine is now, so all is perfect. There is only this place, this time and these conditions. Create your reality now. Plant the seeds and tend the garden of your life. The growing season is now. In this sand, sometimes the waves beat against me or the winds shift the sand beneath me. I grow by learning and adapting. Bending and flowing and finding every condition perfect. This is where I am. This is my life. So I will grow, even in sand."

THE SEA GRASS'S PRAYER

Dearest Divine One, who is the source of all, assist me in experiencing the expansiveness of the Universe. Guide me to be unlimited in all things in all ways. Expand my belief system so that I may live and act in the perfect soil of the now. I AM listening and expressing the expansiveness of my knowing daily. And so it is. Thank you God.

18
LONDON TREE

Autumn 2004. The garden bedded down for winter. The empty arrow of life bed rested again with my hope of roses for the spring. The crisp temperature brought an air of expectation of the first snow, holidays and the traditional preparations. I was going to London. I purchased a ticket and made reservations for a spring trip. I knew this would be a marvelous trip. In my excitement I looked forward to the trip, all the time wondering why was I going to London? This was not a trip I had long thought about and planned. I made the decision to go in a quick moment. After weeks of casual wondering, I asked the question during my meditation. The answer came weeks later when I ended another meditation. I heard "Can you hear me?" I heard this line for several days before it occurred to me to say yes. When I said yes, the rest of the poem flooded my mind.

I am going to London to meet a tree. The tree was in Kensington Gardens. I opened the map of London, found Kensington Gardens and inked in a dot to mark where the tree would be. So that is why I had selected a hotel across the street from the gardens! It all made perfect sense.

LONDON TREE

Can you hear me?
Are you there?
Can you see me?
Are you there?
My roots reach out to touch yours.
My branches stretch to feel your breath
Across the ocean's waters.
I long for your gaze.
I long for your whisper on my bark.
Come to me
Come back to me.
We loved each other once
Lifetimes ago.
Do you remember?
Your arms wrapped around me,
Your face pressed against my trunk,
Whispering secret dreams and fears.
Gathering my strength for yours
Facing the grown up world you turned away.
I am here
I am calling
Remember me
Come to me
Loving you is
My solitary purpose
Can you hear me?

The tree called to me and loved me all winter. By spring, I was anxious to be with the tree.

Spring 2005. It was still below freezing at times and the garden continued to sleep in the safety of the soil's covering. I left the house for London and noted some small green tips in the arrow of life bed. Resting the bed over winter was my strategy to hopefully achieve agreement with Nature to plant roses in the spring. My second spring since building this bed and my second attempt to install roses. In my excitement to start my big trip,

I dismissed the green tips as some early weeds. I was soon in the air full of anticipation and the green plant tips were long forgotten.

As the Heathrow airport shuttle van drove past Kensington Gardens, the trees took my breath away. I felt their powerful energy. They were stately, grand and very old. Elders, I knew they held much knowledge. I checked into the hotel, found my room and opened the drapes and looked across the street to Kensington Gardens. I quickly changed my shoes, packed my map and set out to find my tree, the London Tree. In my walking, I encountered many trees. I met the Gnome Trees and also found the Council of Trees. Soon I found the London Tree. It was very close to spot I had marked on the map last fall.

LONDON TREE 2

Ah
You are here
Your essence, signature on my memory
Lean into me
Energies entwining
And now you remember
A duet of love, melody familiar

I brought my tree a gift of quartz crystals. I placed the crystals in a hollow spot on the tree's trunk. I kissed the tree, leaned against it and studied it from every angle. This was a reunion with a dear one. I was happy. I felt at peace. I visited the tree every day. One afternoon, it was warm and sunny and I sat at the base of the tree cradled between two large roots. As I leaned against the tree, I gazed at a group of trees I recognized as the Council of Trees. These trees were in communion with all the trees in the Gardens and held much wisdom. I felt them acknowledge to my tree that I had indeed come.

COUNCIL OF TREES

Second stanza this duet
Refrain is love
Follow the trees
Deep roots into this Earth

Foundation to soar your spirit
Aim your love towards the Earth
Bless the Earth and hearts of all
Duet of love
Your voice sings
Accompanied by the trees
Amplifying the power of love
Belonging always to you

Time to leave London. I cried saying goodbye to my tree. It was incredibly difficult to leave. I walked around the tree and collected a few sticks lying on the ground. I kissed the tree wondering if I would ever see it again. A few hours later, I sat in the airplane, missing my tree. The power of the tree, its energy and the gentleness of its love, I can feel at any moment. It is true, our energies are entwined forever. I love you London Tree.

LONDON TREE 3

We two are love
Bound forever singing this duet
You wept taking your leave
Not knowing I dwell in you
And you in me
Come to me and I am here
Beyond chains of the physical realm.
Loving you is my solitary purpose
And loving the Earth is yours.
Duet, melody familiar

COMPLETE LONDON TREE

Can you hear me?
Are you here?
Can you see me?
Are you there?
My roots reach out to touch yours.
My branches stretch to feel your breath
Across the ocean's waters.

I long for your gaze.
I long for your whisper on my bark.
Come to me
Come back to me.
We loved each other once
Lifetimes ago.
Do you remember?
Your arms wrapped around me.
Your face pressed against my trunk,
Whispering secret dreams and fears.
Gathering my strength for yours
Facing the grown up world you turned away.
I am here
I am calling
Remember me
Come to me
Loving you is
My solitary purpose
Can you hear me?
Ah
You are here
Your essence, signature on my memory
Lean into me
Energies entwining
And now you remember
A duet of love, melody familiar
We two are love
Bound forever singing this duet
You wept taking your leave
Not knowing I dwell in you
And you in me
Come to me and I am here
Beyond chains of the physical realm.
Loving you is my solitary purpose
And loving the Earth is yours
Duet, melody familiar.

19

THE GNOME TREES

The Gnome Trees in Kensington Gardens, were five trees facing one another, hundreds of years old with gnarled black trunks wider than my outstretched arms. Some of their branches swept low to the ground with many angular joints. Most likely there were six trees at one time because one tree had no partner. I laughed out loud when I spotted the first one. Such a comical collection of characters. They hummed, giggled and danced. I visited the trees almost everyday and enjoyed their comedy.

"You are following me." "I am not moving."

"Not when I look right at you. But I know you are." I turned my back and spun around quickly to catch him moving.

"I am not moving."

"It is silly to try to follow me. You are too big to be sneaky. There is no point in being sneaky when I already know you are following me. I know trees move and walk around all the time."

"No we can't."

"Yes you can. As a little girl at camp I felt trees move into our campfire circle to enjoy our singing, talking and laughing."

"You can't see me moving."

"I hear you humming. You can't be tricky and also hum at the same time."

"You can't see me."

"Yes I can! You are right there." I suspected that though both of us were over fifty years old, neither of us felt that old.

"No I am not. I am hiding. Try to find me."

"OK. 1, 2, 3, ready or not, here I come. A ha! I found you!"

"I thought that was a good hiding place."

"Your humming gave you away."

"Let's play again. Turn around and I will hide."

"OK. Ready? 1, 2, 3. Ready or not, here I come! Hmm." I saw the tree but it wouldn't be fun to find him right away. "Is the tree over there? No. How about over there? Nooooo. Hmmmm. I wonder where the tree could be." The tree's humming was broken by giggling.

"A ha! There you are. I found you! Why do you hum if you want to hide?"

"My heart is full of joy and humming just pops out of me. Is your heart hiding or humming?"

"Both but not at the same time. Sometimes I hide my heart. Protection I guess. My heart hums when I am in a garden and when I touch trees like you."

"Your heart needs no cage. Keeping safe is not being free. Sing your song. You need not words. Sing your path, the melody is your purpose."

"This sounds similar to the London Tree."

"Ahhh. Same song."

Lesson redux.

THE GNOME TREE'S PRAYER

Glorious Universe, where humor and fun originate, I bless you. Lift my spirits and fill me with the spontaneity of a child. My laughter fills the atmosphere with joy. Ease my cares so that I may play with abandon. I AM refreshing my spirit with merriment. And so it is. Thank you God.

20

THE
DAFFODILS

March 2005. When I returned from London, luggage in tow, one daffodil bloomed in the arrow of life bed, surrounded by many others with buds. The green tips I spotted as I left for London were now daffodils.

"Hello! Hello! Hello! Here I am. Happy Happy Spring. Daffodils salute you. Hello!"

"Oh my! You are a daffodil and so many of you are in this bed."

"Hello! A surprise! Magic of Nature surprising you again. I couldn't wait for you to come home. Surprise. You are surprised aren't you?"

"Yes I am. I always wonder how plants I didn't plant sprout and grow." I thought of the cantaloupe. "I can explain that seeds blew in the wind and took hold in the soil. But daffodils grow from bulbs."

"Explaining is your mistake. You and the garden and in fact, the entire earth are not limited by the scientific rules you humans created. Humans created rules like the law of gravity to understand the world. Surprise! The world is not what you think you know. Anything can be. The limits are only what you create. Hello! Hello! You can also create unlimits. Creating unlimits allows you to craft."

"Craft?"

"Like me. Surprise! Hello! Hello!"

"You mean craft like make things?"

"Hellow! Hellow! Yes, craft, invent, and produce, using creative energy to manifest in the physical world. Hello! Hello! I am so happy to be here. This is a wonderful bed. I am calling Hello to all the plants. I am sure when all of us bloom we will be loud enough to wake all the others in the garden. The rose can hear us. The butterfly bush is a sound sleeper."

A few days later we spoke again.

"Hello! Hello! I call Hello to you each time you go by."

"Yes, I hear you every morning on my way to work. You are especially bouncy. I am wondering about unlimits. Creating unlimits as you say is seeing anything as possible?"

"Spring is here. I am so excited to meet all the others. Hello! No, there are humans who say anything is possible but still believe and rely on limits in your world. Creating unlimits is active. You create the space in your world with no limits ever. Hello! I am working right now. Look the hydrangea has some green tips. I am singing and calling Hello all day long. Surprise, I am waking up the garden. Hello! Helloooooo! Wake up to the world.

And you, create unlimits and help the world wake up to us. Hello! Look at me. Yes, it is spring again."

"So I can make a space in my world or life that has no limits and use that spot for my connection to the Universe for creative endeavors?"

"Well you could, but that is limiting. It is limited in space and in its use. A limit is not an unlimit is it? Hello! Hello! Do you prefer Helloooooooooooh! Hellooooooooooooooooo! Or Hellow? Sometimes I like to linger on the O part."

"I like Helloooooh. OK, an unlimit is helping the world realize the gifts the plants, trees and rocks bring to the earth and to us?"

"No. Hellow! That would be the result of the unlimit. A great result I must say. Think how happy we would be if everyone could talk and understand one another. Humans have trouble doing that with other humans. Hello! That is a limit. The big unlimit leads to universal communication with all beings including us. You can help shift the perspective."

"I can start unfreezing the thoughts around plants and nature to start the creation of the unlimit?" I thought if he paid attention to my questions, this conversation could be shorter.

"Yes. Yes. And you need to live in unlimit to create the movement of the shift. I told you once already to create your world with unlimits. You can't heal the earth with limits. Feeling unworthy or too small? Limit! Live in the unlimited. The whole of Nature and the Universe is supporting and funding your purpose. Live in the unlimited energy of the Universe. I am working you know. I am your harbinger of spring. Hellooooo! Spring is here! Some humans use the crocus as the harbinger of spring. I am really delighted I got the job. There are so many plants to wake up in such a small garden. It is astonishing the space looks small and yet you have so many beds and every inch filled with the flora of Nature. And spring is here. Hello and wake up."

"I do appreciate you taking on the job. I always used the forsythia as my harbinger of spring."

"The forsythia is late this year. Harbingers cannot be late. It would not be good form for others in the garden to wake up the harbinger. I can hear the talk now. Hello! Wake up you harbinger, spring is over, and it is summer. Hello! I am here on the job so you now have a proper harbinger. No one has to wake me up." "I didn't plant anything in this bed because I was saving the space for roses this spring."

"And we are here. You know the answer to the roses is no. Daffodils are here now."

"I didn't think the no was a long term forever kind of no. I thought it was no to roses last planting season. I always thought this bed would be wonderful for roses."

Daffodils popping up and foiling roses. Edward must have spent his entire winter creating this grand display. Isn't it interesting that he has been quiet since I returned from London? Of course who in the garden can speak a word with such a loquacious daffodil on the job? Daffodils, my favorite flower saying no to roses. The daffodil interrupted my thoughts.

"Hello! Wake up garden. We daffodils are in this bed now. And we are working all day. Harbinger is a great responsibility. Hellow! Helloooooo."

"Isn't saying no to roses a limit?"

"Twisting words will not create a rose bed. Helloooooooo hydrangea. Your job is to create unlimits. Perhaps in that you can learn how to create the result of roses. I must work now. Hellooooooooo Spring!"

THE DAFFODIL'S PRAYER

Sacred heart of God living within my heart, allow your wisdom to flow in communication with all of my cells in my entire being. And as your unlimited knowledge flows, assist me in reflecting your understanding love and compassion to the world. Wake us up to the eternal spring of love. I AM the expression of God's love and compassion now. And so it is. Thank you God.

21

COREOPSIS AGAIN

Spring 2005. The freezes and frosts were over and planting was now safe. Even though there would be no additional roses, hundred of blossoms carpeted my two rose bushes at the east end of a hosta bed. Their beautiful display made up for the fact I would not have any new roses.

I traveled to the botanical garden's nature reserve in search of new plants. Still no word from Edward. After his impressive conspiracy with the daffodils, I was also quiet. I did admire the daffodil display and the hilarity of the little fellow. And I will never admit that to Edward.

At the reserve, many different growers offered an assortment of indigenous wildflowers. I chose from hundreds of plants fit for sun, partial sun or shade that would thrive in the mid-west prairie. I wandered around enjoying the plants and the choices. While I looked at Virginia blue bells, the grower approached me with a flowerpot in her hand. She asked if I had considered coreopsis for my garden and handed me the container. I smiled at the directness of Nature. This was a message I could not miss. I purchased the plant and added it to the box I carried. I also bought sweet berry and Jacob's ladder seeds.

The sweet berry went in under the dogwood. The coreopsis and Jacob's ladder were planted in the arrow of life bed. The other beds were already full of perennials. I marked the Jacob's ladder seeds with twigs as usual so I could not mistake the seedlings for weeds.

The coreopsis was a new variety. The leaves were delicate and lacy and the yellow flowers were tiny and graceful. I planted it at the pointy end of the arrow bed. Ok Edward, I thought. I have now planted coreopsis two years in a row. Coreopsis, not roses. Does cooperation with Nature mean Nature's way? Where is the teamwork, collaboration, compromise?

"It is all about purpose you know." Edward rocked back and forth on his heels. His pockets bulged. Probably full of daffodil bulbs, I thought.

"I know this year I planted coreopsis on purpose. It was hard to miss the message when someone hands me a flower pot of it."

"Life's purpose. I am talking about discovering your gifts and learning their correct use in following your life's purpose. God's purpose is fulfilled through you. Listen and know your life's purpose and then follow it. The world is filled with spirit as humans discover and act on their purpose. The world is waiting for this part of God that lies within you. What will the world look like after you act on your purpose?"

"I took a deep breath. It sounds as if you are saying that I can change the world by living my life's purpose. That is a very big thought."

"This is not work nor is it hard. Your purpose is easy because it is within you and connecting to it is a joyful activity. Do not be afraid of your greatness. Such a fear keeps you from the world and all that you can do. Fulfilling your purpose in the world blesses all. Fear is of the mind or ego. Any time you disallow the expansion of your purpose, you are in fear. When you move through the fear you will be content and energized. Allowing the nature of things to take place attains happiness and peace. By allowing your nature, your purpose becomes action. And the nature of all things is expansion. It is time to expand your wisdom. Your wisdom must expand beyond yourself and be expressed in the world. The expression is how you follow your purpose. You already know this part of yourself."

"Happy Spring, Edward. I missed you."

THE COREOPSIS' PRAYER

Oh God that I AM resting in your arms, cradle me until I am ready to walk in my purpose. Support my steps as I present the world with my distinctive blessing that only I can offer. I AM a sacred part of God and in my sacredness I consecrate all that is seen and unseen. And so it is. Thank you God.

22
THE
HYDRANGEA

Summer 2005. The hydrangea in my garden grew large snowball shaped blossoms in a variety of blues. From a distance it looked sky blue. On closer inspection, I saw many blues, pale blue to deep violet blue. Each large blossom was comprised of many small florets, each was unique. Each floret became a part of the larger blossom.

"Oneness."

"Oneness?" I took off my garden gloves and sat next to Edward on the brick wall.

"Yes. You are looking at oneness. Each segment merges and becomes a collective. A whole. Oneness. Oneness is all. Most humans do not accept this. Many humans revel in their uniqueness or specialness. It is true, each is unique. A unique spark from God's fire. All sparks are a part of the one flame. This is what humans forget. And returning to the flame or to God, to feel the peace, joy and comfort of being one is the true pursuit of humans. Humans have simply forgotten they are already here."

"We are more than one with one another aren't we? I feel at one with my garden."

"Oneness is all. Oneness is the Universe. All. The earth is a living being. It is true you are one with the garden, Nature and Mother Earth herself. All. All has no limits. Each human, plant, tree, rock and creature are a part of the collective known as Earth. The Earth is part of the collective, the Universe. The Universe is part of the All. That is explaining it in human, linear terms. Each human is part of the All and so is one with All. I mention humans are parts of the collective called Earth because it is now vital humans understand the implications of their actions. A harmful action toward the Earth is a harmful action towards one's self. Humans and the Earth cannot progress in this manner. This separateness is an illusion. It is in this view of separateness that humans create harm. Hurting one is hurting all. The illusion dissolved reveals oneness as the true reality. The power of healing with love can begin. A loving action towards the Earth is a loving action towards one's self. Loving one is loving all. Loving all is loving one. Oneness. Peace, joy, love and comfort are here now in oneness. God is one. God is all. Oneness is all. All."

THE HYDRANGEA'S PRAYER

Heavenly beings please be with me now. Today, help me remember that the One Spirit resides in all of us. This remembrance will guide me in honoring each living being as the creation of God. Seeing my oneness with all creates peace and healing. I AM healing the earth by seeing the perfection of God in everyone and everything. And so it is. Thank you God.

23
THE TOMATO

A tomato sprouted next to the coreopsis. I smiled. That arrow of life bed is no ordinary garden bed, I said to myself. The first time I saw Edward, he told me to build that bed. Cantaloupe, daffodils and now tomatoes. This bed doesn't need a gardener. Plants seem to plant themselves. Edward must enjoy creating these surprises.

I did not stake the tomato instead I allowed it to vine naturally. Soon it covered the arrow of life garden bed and spilled over the garden's sides. The vines produced countless tiny yellow blossoms and pea-sized green tomatoes. The tomato was silent for weeks. I wondered why it was here and what messages it had for me.

"Purposeful warrior." "Where?"

"Here."

"Here? Purposeful warrior? The, tomato, is a purposeful warrior? I always thought tomatoes were rather soft. They bruise so easily how can they be warriors?"

"No. You."

"Me? A warrior? No. No. No. I bruise almost as easily as the tomato."

"Purposeful warrior. A purposeful warrior possesses mental strength and courage to address fears and to proceed. Every time you tell someone about us, you act in courage. You have the courage to dare and share the truth of the garden. Every day brings you the chance to defy your fears about what humans may think regarding your relationship with us."

"I continue to feel I have to be careful where I share it. Wondering about what others think is still a deal for me. I haven't told just anyone about talking to plants. I would like to draw in a deep breath, kick off my fears, and rest in the truth of what I know."

"We are told all we need to know. We find out just in the right time. When you tell someone about us perhaps that person needs to know. When you are afraid, you have just forgotten your connection with God. You are never alone and you never have to do anything alone. Living every breath in God's heart creates the warrior. And you are a purposeful warrior. Offer love through loving the plants and the earth. Others will be attracted to offer love too. And so the love expands. The miracle lies in shifting the mind's perception about the Earth and Nature. There are many ways to God. However, there is only one choice for any of us and it is to be a means of God's love."

I listen to the voice of Nature. In Nature I see the treasures of God's love. There, I feel a deep sense of belonging and oneness with the Earth.

Spring 2006. For the purpose of storytelling, this tale ends. I can assure you the adventure with Edward and the Nature Beings continues. A friend helped me start a Fairy Garden. The garden is entered through a ten-inch-tall arbor with glass buttons for stepping stones. A miniature table set for tea awaits the sprites. An abalone shell filled with water makes an excellent reflecting pool. And I am now discovering miniature plants for the garden. Edward's synchronicity at play again.

Most of the lessons in this story were given to me while in the garden. Gardening is easier than applying some of these lessons. Our wonderful Earth School gives no grades (judgment), has no due dates (only the present moment) and offers us a lifetime to master the lessons.

Let your journey unfold and pay attention to your vision, dream or purpose. Attention allows you to focus your intention on achieving your purpose. Loving attention and intention will harness the universal energy to flow through you to manifest your creation. Love is the creative force in the Universe and precedes all creation. Love can manifest miracles. The moment is now. Each of us has a distinct purpose or gift to offer the world. Only you have it. What would the world miss if you did not live your truth and fulfill your purpose? No one else here has that gift to offer in your absence.

Our purpose or gift honors the Universal Law of Oneness. What is done to one is done to all. No gift is too small. No gift is inconsequential. The moment is now. Say YES.

PRAYER TO THE UNIVERSE

Oh great Universe. I love and adore thee. I offer gratitude for the golden sun, sparkling stars and spinning planets. I bless God's streams of light creating all that is seen and unseen. The light gives life. I love the light and I attend the light that sustains me. And God said let there be light. I AM the light of God. May the light that flows through me create God's living blessing here on Earth. And so it is. Thank you God.

APPENDIX A

COLLECTION OF PRAYERS

THE DANDELION'S PRAYER

Dear Holy Presence, please be with me now and forevermore. Guide my thoughts, words and actions to honor the divine in me and in others. Help me remember that in honoring all others and myself, I honor you. I AM creating, in the fullness of my capacity, love as your Divine intention conceived it to be. And so it is. Thank you God.

THE LAVENDER'S PRAYER

Dearest Divine One! Awaken within me my divine purpose. Set me on this journey. For I now know my purpose is not a destination but a journey. Help me relinquish my human need for control. My safety was never in my control. Embrace me with the safety of peace as I joyfully choose to follow my divine purpose with all of my beingness. I AM walking my divine path in the fullness of God, one step at a time. And so it is. Thank you God.

THE LOVING TREE'S PRAYER

Most beautiful Mother Earth who is at one with God, thank you for the beauty of your presence, dressed and decorated by Nature. I see God's love in the beauty of your waters, flowers and trees. Still my mind and open my heart to the complete expression of love. Through love, I AM creating that which I wish to be. I AM love. And so it is. Thank you Mother Earth. Thank you God.

THE LILAC'S PRAYER

Oh most Holy Father-Mother God, how great thou art! As May brings the Lilac into full bloom and perfumes the world to remind us of its transformation, bring to our minds the present. Open our hearts so we sense and perceive the transformation of humanity. As we perceive what is possible, open our vision so that we see from the whole and are not limited by our own viewpoint. Guide us in this vision to create the will to transform ourselves into the most holy images of God. And as the new seeks to emerge, grant us courage to embody and live our presence now. And so it is. Thank you God.

THE JUNIPER'S PRAYER

I AM calling forth to my Guardian Angel, the loving one assisting me with my journey. Help me recognize that events and experiences occur in my life in perfect order, each serving as the foundation for the next. Help me release judgment in this process, remembering it does not serve me to compare my path to another's. Rest my curious mind with the peace that my journey will unfold in its natural way. Tune my listening so that instead of trying to direct my path, I may hear directions while on my path. Open my eyes to see the miracles in the synchronicity of events. Expand my heart's delight with this journey. And so it is. Thank you God.

THE CHRISTMAS ROSE'S PRAYER

Dearest Holy Infant please hear my prayer as my heart sends it upward to the heavens on tiny pink rose petals wrapped in the blessing of peace. Thank you for joy which softens the harshness of winter. Please bestow a blessing on each being walking this earth that all will know peace. Open every heart so that all may become creators of peace. May we master this art on earth as it is in the heavens. Keep me mindful of cherishing peace in the joy of this life. And so it is. Thank you God.

THE MOONFLOWER'S PRAYER

To the angels and heavenly hosts whom I love in the truth, I call for your assistance. If I have lost my true self; help me reconnect. If I have forgotten my true self; remind me. If I cannot see my true self; show me. Ignite in me a passion for living my truth in every way, everyday. As my passion grows, my spirit is at peace. I AM living authentically as my true self, a divine spark from God. And so it is. Thank you God.

THE CANTALOUPE'S PRAYER

Father, Father, Father, be with me now. You have said everything is possible for he who believes. Seal this truth in my heart of hearts. Connect my heart to my mind so that I may know this always. Awaken my mind and my heart should I ever question a possibility. Instill in me joyful imagination as I delight in the possibility of my life and the world. I AM dwelling in the sacred privilege of my possibilities and choices. And so it is. Thank you God.

THE DAY LILY'S PRAYER

Flowers of the heavenly hosts, salutations! Thank you for your beauty here on Earth. Open my heart to my highest presence. Assist me in knowing and trusting my true and real self. Remind me to revel in the beauty of my love and my gifts so that in my awe I may see their value to the world. I AM worthy of giving and receiving God's beautiful love. And so it is. Thank you God.

THE SEA'S PRAYER

Neptune and all of the Universe's spirit guides of the sea, strengthen my vigilance and resolve so I remain constant and faithful in my word. May my word, my promises, be as mighty as the sea whose presence is never questioned. As each promise kept washes over me in a wave of love, I AM fortified. And so it is. Thank you God.

THE WIND'S PRAYER

Winds of God, breath of God, from whom all grace and good proceed, be with me now. I beseech thee to protect me from my human limitations. Preserve my devotion to you when I am distracted by earthly fixations. Strengthen me to stand and receive thy blessings so that I may change my human ways and magnify thy love and greatness forever. And so it is. Thank you God.

THE SEA GRASS'S PRAYER

Dearest Divine One, who is the source of all, assist me in experiencing the expansiveness of the Universe. Guide me to be unlimited in all things in all ways. Expand my belief system so that I may live and act in the perfect soil of the now. I AM listening and expressing the expansiveness of my knowing daily. And so it is. Thank you God.

THE GNOME TREE'S PRAYER

Glorious Universe, where humor and fun originate, I bless you. Lift my spirits and fill me with the spontaneity of a child. My laughter fills the atmosphere with joy. Ease my cares so that I may play with abandon. I AM refreshing my spirit with merriment. And so it is. Thank you God.

THE DAFFODIL'S PRAYER

Sacred heart of God living within my heart, allow your wisdom to flow in communication with all of my cells in my entire being. And as your unlimited knowledge flows, assist me in reflecting your understanding love and compassion to the world. Wake us up to the eternal spring of love. I AM the expression of God's love and compassion now. And so it is. Thank you God.

THE COREOPSIS' PRAYER

Oh God that I AM resting in your arms, cradle me until I am ready to walk in my purpose. Support my steps as I present the world with my distinctive blessing that only I can offer. I AM a sacred part of God and in my sacredness I consecrate all that is seen and unseen. And so it is. Thank you God.

THE HYDRANGEA'S PRAYER

Heavenly beings please be with me now. Today, help me remember that the One Spirit resides in all of us. This remembrance will guide me in honoring each living being as the creation of God. Seeing my oneness with all creates peace and healing. I AM healing the earth by seeing the perfection of God in everyone and everything. And so it is. Thank you God.

PRAYER TO THE UNIVERSE

Oh great Universe. I love and adore thee. I offer gratitude for the golden sun, sparkling stars and spinning planets. I bless God's streams of light creating all that is seen and unseen. The light gives life. I love the light and I attend the light that sustains me. And God said let there be light. I AM the light of God. May the light that flows through me create God's living blessing here on Earth. And so it is. Thank you God.

APPENDIX B

HOW TO CONNECT WITH NATURE A GUIDED MEDITATION

HOW TO CONNECT WITH NATURE A GUIDED MEDITATION

Talking with plants starts with an attitude of love and belief we are all connected. This interconnectedness embraces everyone and everything in the environment. It is the core of harmony with the world. A plant's physical and genetic makeup, its chemical constituents, personality and spirit all present a picture depicting the plant's identity.

Trust your intuition and quiet your mind and body. Ask the plant for permission to commune with it and receive its blessings. Listen and act on your intuition. Plants usually are very willing to share their knowledge and gifts. If something does not feel genuine then stop. It could be that you are not yet ready to take the journey with the plant.

Once you have received permission from the plant. Gently touch it with your hands. Close your eyes and take several long, deep cleansing breaths. Inhale deeply and imagine long roots growing from your tailbone or feet deep into the earth. This will ground you. Continue to breathe deeply, imagining your breath going down your roots into the earth. Once you feel you are breathing into the earth, slowly release your breath through your mouth with an audible sigh.

Continue to inhale deeply and imagine you are breathing into the earth and exhale through your mouth and imagine the earth's energy going into the air. Repeat this sequence several times until you feel relaxed and mindless and then return to your normal rhythm of breathing. Thoughts may cross your mind and if they do just let the thought go. Return your attention to your breath. Keeping your focus and awareness on your breath helps calm your mind.

Imagine your roots connecting to the plant's roots. Breathe in a relaxed easy way. Imagine the roots becoming more connected until you feel you are the plant's roots. This is called becoming. Notice how you feel. How as the plant's roots do you grow and move? What color are you? Is there any odor or fragrance to the roots? Now move up and become the plant's stem. How does it feel? Is the stem sturdy and strong or wispy thin? Can you feel yourself moving in the breeze? Do you have branches? Travel down the branch. Does the branch feel different from the stem? Travel to the place where the leaves attach to the stem. Journey into the leaf. How do you connect to the stem? What is your shape and texture? How do the leaves position themselves? What is their relationship to each other? Continue to go where spirit takes you. Travel to a flower blossom. Explore the hidden places of the flower, the petals and stamen. Where are your facing as the blossom? Are you looking up, down or tracking the sun? Notice how you are feeling. Does your energy as the plant feel different from your energy as a human being?

Listen for the Nature Spirit of the plant. Listen. Human thought is an obstacle to hearing the plant or tree. Go beyond thought to feeling and empathy. Welcome the plant to talk with you. Listen and ask questions much like you would when getting to know a new person. Keep your mind open and quiet so you can hear what it has to say. Maintain an attitude of the pupil, learning from the plant.

When you feel complete, travel back down to the roots. See your roots separating from the plant's roots. Thank the plant for the journey and the blessings. Take deep breaths and follow your breath up from your roots to the base of your tailbone or feet, wherever your roots originated. Take a few more deep breaths and gradually open your eyes.

To connect with a rock, hold the rock in your hand and become it. If the rock is too big, hold it in your heart. Get to know the rock by studying its physical characteristics. Enter the common space you both share, the spiritual realm. Relax into the qualities of the rock and become one. Concentrate on sending it love from your heart. See a loving light leaving your heart center and enveloping the rock. Each rock has its own character as well as each individual plant within a species. When you communicate with a plant or a rock, you are communicating with the spirit or deva. For example, the deva of all the daisies will speak to you through an individual daisy.

Write your experience with the plant or rock and noting any messages you received. It is helpful to keep a journal of your Nature connections. You may find the messages have a common theme or contain lessons that build one on the next. A journal will assist you in using this information for your highest good. Pay attention to how you feel and if you feel any sensation or impact in any particular part of your body. Write the affirmations the plant or rock may have given to you. Read, sing or chant the affirmation out loud.

Plants, trees and rocks are a means to connect to God. Opening your heart and mind to the energy of the plant or rock creates the connection to nature and to the energy of the divine.

APPENDIX C

HOW TO MAKE AND USE A FLOWER ESSENCE

HOW TO MAKE AND USE A FLOWER ESSENCE

Dr. Edward Bach (1886-1936) developed flower essences in England during the 1920's and 30's. Although trained as a traditional western medical physician, Dr. Bach developed and utilized his intuition in his healing practice. He believed that physical diseases are symptoms of an ailing heart and/or spirit. He thought fear and anxieties opened a path to illness. Dr. Bach developed a branch of herbal medicine using only flowers, the vital energy of the plant, to relieve distress. When someone is treated with a flower essence, the positive life force energy of the flower helps the person to remove or transform the negative internal energy. When the negative internal energy is replaced by the flower's essence, the mind and body recognize this positive energy as the natural and desired state of the human. This serves to remind the body/mind that positive life force energy is what it should be creating and allowing to ensure a healthy body and mind. The life force energy of the flower essence is a way to connect to the universal life force energy.

Flower essences are a vibration of the flower's energy and can be used for physical, emotional, mental or spiritual well-being. When taking the flower essence it is important to know the remedy's purpose and be clear about your intention regarding the remedy. A clear intention creates a powerful relationship with the flower essence and potentiates the effects.

Warning. The recipe and directions for flower essences is provided for your information. The author is not providing medical advice. This information should not be construed as an attempt to engage in the practice of medicine. If you suspect you may have a health problem you should consult your healthcare provider. Never disregard professional medical advice or delay seeking it because of something you read. If you think you may have a medical emergency, call your doctor or 911 immediately.

Supplies

FLOWER ESSENCE RECIPE

Clear glass bowl about 3 or 4 inches deep
Purified or spring water
Two stones or crystals to separate the flower from the stem
Brandy or cider vinegar for preservative
Two 1-2 ounce amber or dark glass bottles

It is best to make your flower essence under a sunny sky with no clouds. However, you may wish to experiment with cloudy skies or moonlight for different effects.

Locate a flower that appeals to you. Flowers in full bloom show the plant's energy and expression. Sit near the plant and give thanks to the plant for giving you this flower and its vital energy.

Fill the glass bowl with the spring water and using stones or crystals cut the blossom from the stem. Allow the flower to drop into the bowl. Do not touch the flower or the water. Let the bowl steep in the sunlight for about 3 hours or until the flower begins to wilt. If you are using moonlight, the flowers can steep for 4 hours or even all night.

Connect to the plant and flower through becoming as described in the previous appendix. Experience oneness with the plant and listen for its gifts that will be present in the flower essence. When the essence has been captured in the water, strain the water into a bottle and label it as the mother tincture.

When you return home, put 4–10 drops of the mother tincture into a sterilized bottle, fill the bottle to one-third with brandy or cider vinegar as the preservative and two-thirds with spring water. Keep in a cool, dry place and avoid sunlight. I store my flower essences in the refrigerator. This concentrated form of the essence is your stock bottle. To make the remedy elixir, sterilize a one-ounce bottle and put 2 to 4 drops of the mother tincture in the bottle filled with one third brandy or cider vinegar and two thirds spring water.

To take the flower remedy, place 2 to 4 drops from the elixir bottle under the tongue or in a cup of water four times a day for a week or as long as necessary. Listen and rely on your intuition and stop the remedy when you feel the desired energetic shift or change. Homeopathy relies on the principle of less is more. It is more important to take the drops consistently with clear intention than to take many drops.

Flower essences, herbal remedies, essential oils remind us of our relationship to Mother Earth and to the Universe. We are all one. Honoring and caring for the plants of the Earth is the same as honoring and caring for ourselves. Plants offer us food, medicine, healing and the oxygen we breathe. We cannot live without plants however, they can live very well without us.

NAVAJO PROVERB

I have been to the end of the earth.
I have been to the end of the waters.
I have been to the end of the sky.
I have been to the end of the mountains.
I have found none that are not my friends.

The End of this story for now.

www.ingramcontent.com/pod-product-compliance
Lightning Source LLC
Chambersburg PA
CBHW031427120626
46545CB00006B/2303